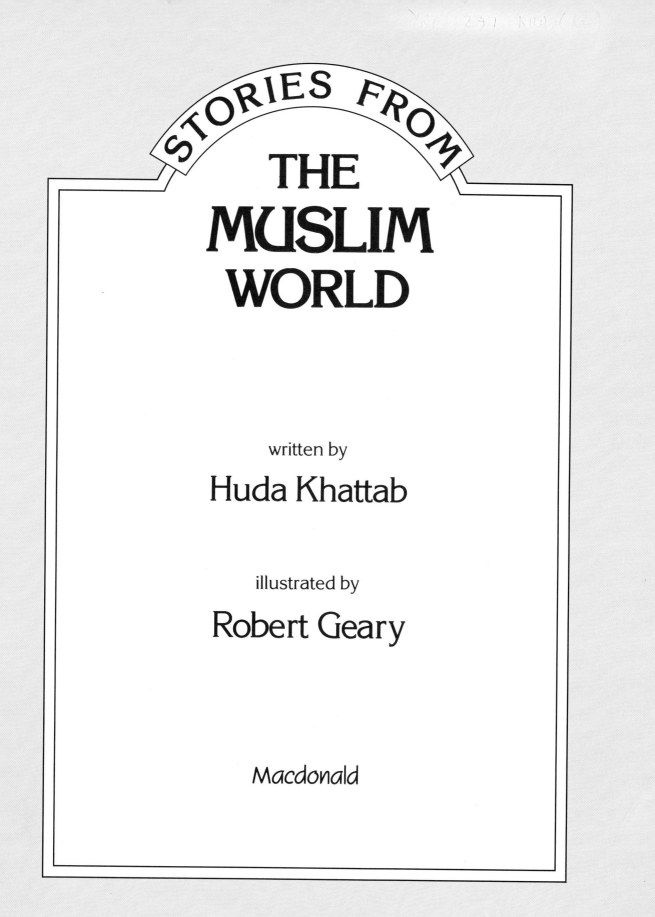

STORIES FROM
THE
MUSLIM
WORLD

written by

Huda Khattab

illustrated by

Robert Geary

Macdonald

Managing Editor : Belinda Hollyer
Book Editors : Barbara Tombs, Jenny Vaughan
Designer : Liz Black
Production Controller : Rosemary Bishop

Consultant : Zahra Jazayeri

A MACDONALD BOOK

© text Huda Khattab 1987
© illustrations Macdonald & Co (Publishers) Ltd 1987

First published in Great Britain in 1987 by
Macdonald & Co (Publishers) Ltd
London & Sydney
A BPCC plc company

Printed in Great Britain by
Purnell Book Production Ltd
Member of the BPCC Group

Macdonald & Co (Publishers) Ltd
Greater London House
Hampstead Road
London NW1 7QX

British Library Cataloguing in Publication Data
Khattab, Huda
    Stories from the Muslim world.
    1. Islam — Juvenile literature
    I. Title
    297   BP161.2

    ISBN 0-356-11563-1

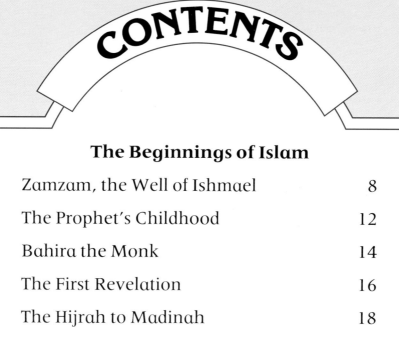

CONTENTS

The Beginnings of Islam

Muslims in History

Muslim Tales

Zamzam, the Well of Ishmael

The story of Abraham is well known to Jews and Christians as well as to Muslims. In Islam he is remembered as one of the great Prophets, and as the father of the Prophet Ishmael, who was the ancestor of Muhammad himself.

Long, long ago, a child was born to the Prophet Abraham and his second wife, Hagar. The baby's name was Ishmael and, when he was born, he was Abraham's only son.

In those days, it was not unusual for a man to have two wives. Abraham's first wife was named Sarah. She had no children, and this made her sad.

But God told Abraham that one day, Sarah too would have a son. He would be named Isaac. Ishmael and Isaac were to be the ancestors of two great nations, the Arabs and the Jews. From these two nations would come three great prophets, Moses, Jesus and Mohammad.

God told Abraham to take Hagar and Ishmael to a new land, far from their home in Palestine. They were to travel through the desert, to a place that God would show them. Abraham knew that the journey would be long and dangerous — but he also knew that he should trust God, who would look after them and provide them with everything they needed.

They set out across the desert, and travelled for many days. At last, they came to a desolate valley. It was the place where, long ago, Adam had built the first place for the worship of the One God. But there was nothing there now but hot sand and bare hills. It was a frightening and lonely place – and yet it seemed to Abraham that this was the place where God wanted him to leave Hagar and her child.

Abraham gave them a little food and water, and prepared to leave. Hagar watched him, afraid of what might happen.

'How can you leave us here?' she cried. 'We will soon have nothing to eat or drink!'

Abraham was too sad to answer.

'Is this God's will, or your own decision?' asked Hagar.

'It is God's command,' replied Abraham.

'In that case, He will take care of us,' replied Hagar.

But at first, it almost seemed as if this was not so. Abraham left, praying as he did so that his family would be safe. It was not long before the food and water were finished. The hot sun beat down on the mother and child. The desert was lonely and silent.

Hagar looked up at the two hills that enclosed the valley. There was not a tree nor a blade of grass, or any living thing in sight. Nothing moved. There was not even a bird in the sky.

The baby began to cry, and the sound tore at Hagar's heart. She knew she must find water. She ran up one of the hills, and scanned the country around for signs of an oasis. She saw nothing. She tried the other hill – but still found nothing.

All the time, Hagar could hear the child crying, and she could not bear it. She ran back to comfort him.

He lay on the ground, kicking the sand with his feet. And as he did so, quite suddenly, water began to gush from the ground. It tumbled quickly over the stones, cutting through the desert sand in a cool, clear stream.

At once, Hagar gave thanks to God, and then gave little Ishmael some water to drink. He stopped crying, and slept peacefully in her arms.

Hagar looked up again at the sky, and saw that flocks of birds were making their way towards the well. They settled by the side of the stream to drink.

Far away, desert travellers saw the birds, and knew they were making for water. They followed the birds, and they too came to the valley and the stream. They saw what a peaceful place it was, and settled there. This was the beginning of the great city of Makkah.

The waters of Zamzam still flow today for the pilgrims who make the holy journey to Makkah. Pilgrims remember the story of Hagar and her baby as they run between the two hills of Safa and Marwa, the hills that Hagar herself ran over in her desperate search. As they run, they pray that God will provide for them too, as He provided for Hagar and Ishmael.

The Prophet's Childhood

The Prophet Muhammad was born in the year 570 CE, in the city of Makkah. His mother's name was Amina, and his father's was Abdullah. Sadly, Abdullah died, leaving Amina a widow even before her child was born.

They say that on the night the Prophet was born, a great star appeared in the sky, and that the child's grandfather, Abd al-Muttalib spent six days deciding on a name for the child. On the seventh day, he dreamed that the name should be Muhammad, which means 'The Praised One'. When he went to tell the baby's mother, he found that she too had had the same dream. And so they named the child.

It was the custom at the time for the women of the city to send their young children into the desert oasis area of Taif, where most of the farms were fertile and the food was good. The children would grow healthy and strong while they were there. The desert women used to come into town and collect the young children – together with payment for the task.

But Amina was a widow, with very little money. It seemed that no one would take her child.

At last a poor woman named Halima agreed to take the child. She already had a child of her own – a son about the same age as Muhammad.

As she travelled home, she wondered how she could feed the children – for her land was poor and all her crops were withered and dry. But she believed that, if she took this child, Allah would bless her.

Her prayers were answered. When she returned to the desert, and her little plot of land, a wonderful sight met her eyes. For the dry, poor earth she had left behind was flourishing. Her fields were full of wheat, ripening in the sun. The trees in her orchard were laden with fruit and there were three times as many goats as there had been when she left. The sheep and camels were producing milk for the first time in years. Both the children grew strong and healthy.

Time passed, and after three years Halima took the child back to his mother in the city of Makkah.

When he was six, his mother took him on another journey – this one to Yathrib, which is now known as Madinah. The family had relatives there, and it was a happy time. But tragedy soon came again, for Amina died on the journey home. Now her child was an orphan, left in the care of his grandfather, Abd al-Muttalib, the man who had given him his name.

Bahira the Monk

There was once a monk named Bahira, who lived in a monastery near the desert city of Busra. He had spent his life in study, and read of a great Prophet who would one day come into the world. Bahira prayed that he would live to see him.

The people of Makkah were merchants, who traded with the cities of Syria. Day after day, caravans of camels, laden with goods, set out across the barren desert. One of these caravans belonged to Abu Talib.

Abu Talib was the Prophet's uncle, and cared for the child now that he had lost both his parents and his grandfather too. One day, Abu Talib decided that Muhammad should travel with him to Syria.

The caravan made its slow way across the desert until, after many days, it reached the edge of the city of Busra.

The monk, seated alone in his cell, looked up from his books, and out across the desert. Through the shimmering heat, he saw a caravan approaching. Above it, a solitary cloud hovered.

14

It seemed that the cloud was shielding someone from the sun. Bahira watched as the caravan drew nearer, and stopped beneath a grove of trees. As soon as everyone was in the shade, the cloud disappeared.

Bahira went to greet the merchants, who he had met before.

'It's good to see you again,' they told him. 'But why do you never invite us into your cell?'

At once, Bahira asked them to join him for a meal. He knew that there was someone very important with them – for what else could the cloud mean? He asked them questions about themselves, but he could not get the answers he wanted. At last he said:

'Are all of your group here?'

'No,' replied Abu Talib. 'My nephew is minding the camels. He's very young, so we didn't bring him.'

'Let me talk to him,' said Bahira.

Bahira questioned the child closely, learning all he could about who he was, what he believed and what he thought. He became sure that Muhammad was the Prophet he was waiting for. He tried one last test.

In this, he asked the child to swear by the idol-gods of Makkah, Lat and Ozza. Muhammad refused.

Bahira spoke at once to Abu Talib:

'This child is destined for greatness,' he said. 'Take him back to your country and look after him well.'

So as soon as he had finished trading in Syria, Abu Talib took his nephew back to Makkah, and looked after him there until he grew up.

15

The First Revelation

The Qur'an is the Holy Book of the Muslims, for whom it is the word of God, set down as it was told to the Prophet Muhammad by the Archangel Gabriel. This is the story of the first time the Prophet heard the words of God.

Muhammad grew up in Makkah, where he married Khadija, a wealthy widow.

At the time, the people of Makkah worshipped idols, but Muhammad was different. He believed in only one God.

He often used to leave the bustling city streets to go away to a cave where he could pray in peace.

The cave was in Mount Hira, just outside the city. It was the Prophet's custom to spend the month of Ramadan there, praying and fasting.

It was during this month, when the Prophet was forty years old, that the Archangel Gabriel appeared to him in the cave, and commanded: 'Read!'

'I cannot read!' stammered the Prophet, for like many people at that time, he could neither read nor write.

Then the Angel embraced the Prophet, holding him so tightly that he thought he would faint. Just when he thought he could bear it no longer, the Angel released him, and commanded him again: 'Read!'

'I cannot read,' the Prophet repeated.

A second time, the Angel embraced the Prophet and commanded him to read – but the reply was the same. Then after a third embrace, the Angel said:

'Read! In the name of thy Lord, who createth,
Createth man from a drop of blood.
Read: and thy Lord is Most Generous:
Who teacheth man the use of the pen,
And teacheth him that which he knew not before.'

Muhammad repeated these words, and knew that he would never forget them. But he was very much afraid, and as soon as he thought he was alone again, he ran from the cave and rushed towards the city.

As he ran, he heard the voice once more:

'Oh, Muhammad, you are the Messenger of Allah, and I am Gabriel.'

He stood still, and looked up. The Archangel stood on the horizon before him, so huge that his figure filled the sky. And whichever way Muhammad turned, the Angel towered before him.

By the time Muhammad had reached his home and his wife, he was shaking with fear. She wrapped him in a blanket, and he told her what had happened.

Khadija knew the story was important – but she did not know what it meant. So she sought out her cousin Waraqa, who was a wise and learned Christian.

'It is the same message that Allah sent to Moses,' Waraqa told her. 'It means that Muhammad is the Prophet of our people. Tell him to be of good cheer.'

But later, he met the Prophet at the Ka'aba, the holy place in Makkah, and he gave him this warning:

'No man has ever brought the message you bring without being opposed. They will call you a liar, and they will cast you out and fight against you. Truly, if I live to see that day, I will help you all I can.'

The Hijrah to Madinah

The festival of Hijrah marks the beginning of the Islamic New Year. The word 'hijrah' means departure, and it is a time when Muslims remember how the Prophet Muhammad left Makkah and made the journey across the desert to Madinah.

The Prophet Muhammad lived in the city of Makkah, where he taught the new religion of Islam. For some time, he had the protection of his powerful uncle Abu Talib. He needed this, as there were many enemies of the new faith living in Makkah. The leaders of an important tribe, the Quraysh, were plotting against him, and when Abu Talib died, the Prophet was in great danger.

At that time, the people of the city of Yathrib (later called Madinah) decided to ask Muhammad to be their governor. There were already a number of Muslims living in Yathrib, many of whom had fled from Makkah.

But the Prophet himself could not leave, for fear of being seen by his enemies. He remained in the city, with his friend Abu Bakr and his young cousin Ali.

The plotters met together, and considered ways of killing the Prophet. But they knew that whoever killed him would be in danger – for the Prophet's own family would be bound to take revenge. At last a man named Abu Jahl spoke up:

'Let each clan among us send a young, strong man to wait outside the Prophet's house this evening. They must stay there all night and in the morning, when he comes out, they must all strike him at once. The Prophet's family will not be able to take revenge on all the men and all their clans.'

But, that very night, the Angel Gabriel warned the Prophet not to sleep in his own home. The Prophet understood that there was a plot against him, so he asked Ali to sleep in his house instead. He promised that no harm would come to him.

As darkness fell, the young men gathered in the shadows near the house. They waited in silence through the night until, at dawn, the door swung open. The attackers sprang forward – and stopped. For instead of the Prophet, they saw Ali. They had been tricked! Enraged, they began at once to make new plans to catch the Prophet.

But he, meanwhile had met with Abu Bakr, who stood ready with two swift camels. It was time to leave Makkah. They set off at once, riding south.

This in itself was a trick, since Yathrib lay to the north of the city, but they knew they must confuse their enemies.

They came to a mountain named Thawr, where they stopped and hid in a cool, quiet cave.

But as soon as the Quraysh realized the Prophet had escaped, they began to search in every direction. They set out across the desert, and even now, they were drawing near to the cave.

The Prophet and Abu Bakr could hear them, close to their hiding place. They stayed still and very quiet, listening hard. The prophet assured Abu Bakr that God would protect them.

'This looks like the sort of place where they might hide,' said a voice, just outside the cave entrance. 'Look! A cave. They're probably in here.'

'Don't be silly,' said another voice. 'No one's been in there for a long time. There's a spider's web right over the entrance – and look, here's a dove, nesting on this ledge. She wouldn't still be sitting there if there were people about. . .'

Abu Bakr heard the party move away. When at last he was sure they had gone, he turned to the Prophet. 'What has happened?' he asked, puzzled. 'There was no spider and no dove when we came in!'

But the Prophet just smiled.

A few days later, when at last it was safe to leave the cave, they made their way to Yathrib, where the Muslims welcomed them. The city became known as Madinat al-Nabi, which means the 'City of the Prophet'. Today it is usually simply known as al-Madinah – 'The City'.

As for the journey, the Hijrah to Madinah, that marked a most important time. For all over the world, Muslims mark that time as the very beginning of their calendar, the first day of the first year of Islam.

Salman the Persian

Salman was a Persian, from a rich and noble family. He could have stayed at home and lived a comfortable life. But instead, he chose to travel the world in search of knowledge of God, first by becoming a Christian, later as a Muslim.

Salman had been travelling for many years, seeking knowledge from holy men wherever he went. He had reached the town of Yathrib (now called Madinah), and was far from home. He was no longer wealthy; indeed, he was very poor, for he had been captured and sold into slavery.

Yet Salman was happy. For he had at last met a wise Christian teacher who had told him that he was soon to meet a great Prophet, who would tell him the truth about God. This Prophet, Salman's teacher had said, would be found in a town where there were many palm trees and which lay between two black hills. In all his travels, Salman had found only one such place – and that was Yathrib.

Every day, as he worked among his master's date palms, under the hot Arabian sun, Salman reminded himself that his teacher had told him how to recognize the Prophet. There would be three signs.

Firstly, if Salman were to offer the Prophet food as alms, he would not eat it. (Alms are something given to the poor, as an offering.) The second sign was that, if the Prophet were given food as a gift, he would eat it. Thirdly, the Prophet would bear a birthmark, called the Seal of Prophecy, between his shoulders.

One day, Salman was working right at the top of a date palm. From there he could see all the countryside – as far as the distant hills, and all along the road to nearby Quba'. A man was running along that road, and Salman recognized him as his master's cousin.

The man seemed very excited. He came running into the orchard, so breathless he could barely speak.

'Have you heard?' he cried. 'There's a great crowd gathering in Quba'. A man has arrived from Makkah – and he says he's a prophet!'

Salman could hardly believe his ears. He scrambled down the palm tree at once, slipping and sliding until he reached the ground. The words tumbled from his mouth – he had asked the man at least a dozen questions before his master shouted at him, angrily:

'Get back up that tree, slave!'

So Salman returned to the top of the date palm and carried on with his work of cutting off the ripe fruit. But his mind was on other things. He knew that he must go to Quba' and see the man from Makkah.

That night, Salman took his ration of dates, and made the journey to Quba'. There, he found the man they called the Prophet, seated with his companions, around a glowing fire.

Salman reached out and gave the Prophet the dates, saying that they were offered as alms.

The Prophet took the dates and handed them to his companions. He took none for himself. That was the first sign!

A few days later, the Prophet came to Yathrib. Once again, Salman crept out of his master's house by night, carrying his ration of dates. Once again, he offered them to the Prophet – only this time he said:

'I offer these not as alms, but as a gift.'

The Prophet took some dates for himself, and offered the rest to his companions. That was the second sign!

Salman soon had a chance to look for the third sign. One of the Prophet's companions died, and there was a funeral. When the prayers were over, Salman greeted the Prophet, who noticed how Salman seemed to be trying to peer at his back. He knew why, and he let his cloak drop from his shoulders so that Salman could see the Seal of Prophecy.

At once, Salman began to weep with joy. He told the Prophet how he had travelled from his home in Persia, through many lands, and now, at last, he had found what he was searching for. All he wanted to do was to spend his life in the service of the Prophet.

But that seemed impossible. For, as a slave, he had to buy his freedom, and his master asked a high price.

'Of course you may leave,' he smiled. 'But first, you must plant three hundred palm trees. Plant them well, for none of them must die. And after that you must pay me.' He named a large sum.

But Salman's faith was rewarded. The Prophet himself came to help Salman plant the trees, bringing his companions with him. The job was soon done – and all the trees lived. Only the money remained to be paid.

The Prophet took a piece of gold, the size of an egg. He had been given it a long time before. It was worth exactly the sum the master demanded. Salman was free at last! And from then onwards, Salman spent his life in the service of the Prophet.

Bilal, the First Muezzin

Bilal was one of the first Muslims. He was the son of a Christian princess from Yemen. She was captured by the pagan rulers of Makkah, and eventually fell in love with an African slave named Riah. They had one child, whose name was Bilal.

Wherever you travel in the Muslim world, you will hear, five times a day, echoing across the housetops, the Call to Prayer. This is the moment when a person called a muezzin, whose task it is to make the call, climbs the minaret (the tower on a mosque). Praising God, he calls the faithful to come to pray.

The first Muslim to make this Call to Prayer was Bilal, the son of an African slave.

In those days, the children of slaves remained slaves themselves. Bilal worked for Umaya, one of the most important men among the pagans of Makkah.

Now, Bilal was a Muslim who believed in only One God. But Umaya was a harsh man, who would not allow his slaves to follow any religion other than his own – which was the worship of idols. Umaya decided to force Bilal to give up Islam.

He had Bilal taken out of the city every day at noon and made to lie on the scorching desert sand under the burning sun. Then he placed a huge stone on top of his chest.

'You'll stay like that,' he said to Bilal, 'until you either die or renounce your religion.'

But Bilal could not deny his faith.

The sun burned down, and the vultures wheeled overhead. Bilal's mouth was dry and the pain in his chest made it almost impossible for him to breathe.

'One God, One God,' he whispered. His master kicked him furiously.

At that moment, Abu Bakr appeared. Abu Bakr was a rich Muslim, a friend and follower of the Prophet – and had himself taught Bilal his religion. He was shocked to see what Umaya was doing to the slave.

'Do you not fear God?' asked Abu Bakr. 'How can you treat the poor man like this?'

'He's my slave. I'll treat him any way I like,' replied Umaya. 'Anyway, this is all because of your interference. You were the one who taught him your religion. You save him! Buy him now if you like!'

And indeed, Abu Bakr did so at once.

Bilal was a devoted follower of the Prophet. After he had been freed he was among those Muslims who later fled from Makkah to Madinah. (You can read about this on page 18.)

The Muslims built a mosque almost as soon as they arrived in Madinah. When it was finished, they considered the ways they could summon the people to prayer. The Christians used a bell, the Jews a horn. Perhaps they should use a clapper, or a drum, a trumpet or a flag? Yet none of these ideas seemed quite right.

Then one of the Prophet's Helpers, Abdullah bin Zaid said: 'Oh, Messenger of God, I have had a dream, in which I heard a man's voice calling us to prayer.'

'Your dream comes from God,' the Prophet told him. 'It shall be so.'

But now they must decide – which man would have this honour? The Prophet laid his hand on Bilal's shoulder.

'Yours is the voice, Bilal,' he said.

Bilal looked around. Everyone was watching him.

'Yours is the best voice,' said the Prophet. And everyone knew it to be so. Bilal had a rich, strong voice, the finest among them.

'But what shall I say?' asked Bilal.

'Praise God, tell the people Muhammad is his messenger and call them to prayer,' said the Prophet. 'That will be enough.'

Today, each mosque has a minaret from which the Call to Prayer is made. But there was no minaret tower on that first mosque, and Bilal had to scramble up the wall and on to the roof of a nearby mud house.

Once there, he looked down at the people around the mosque. He saw the Prophet raise his hands, telling him to begin.

Bilal raised his voice, threw back his head and, for the first time in the history of Islam, uttered the Call to Prayer:

'Allahu akbar, God is most Great.
I witness that there is no God but God.
I witness that Muhammad is the messenger of God.
Come to prayer. Come to good work.'

From then on, until the Prophet's death, Bilal woke him every day for morning prayers, and then called the people from the roof-top near the mosque.

When the Prophet died, Bilal was so stricken with grief that his legs failed him, and he was unable to stand on the roof and make the Call to Prayer. Instead others had to do it for him.

Since then, Islam has travelled to many lands, and the Call to Prayer rings out over many cities – five times a day from Morocco to Indonesia, and wherever there are Muslims. And Bilal, the son of an African, is remembered, honoured and loved by Muslims the world over.

Rabia the Slave

Rabia was a mystic, or a holy woman, who spent her whole life in devotion to God. She was born over a thousand years ago, in the city of Basra, in Iraq.

Long ago, in the city of Basra, there lived a young woman named Rabia. She came from a poor family. She and her three sisters suffered greatly, for their parents had died and then there was a great famine.

It was a violent and dangerous time. The famine made people cruel, ready to do almost anything to survive. Rabia knew it was not safe to walk alone in the town, but she had to find food. One evening, she slipped out of the house, and into the street.

Suddenly, someone caught her, holding her roughly. A hand was over her mouth – she could not cry for help. She had been captured by a wicked dealer in slaves, who then sold her in the market, for just a few coins.

As a slave, Rabia served in the house of a rich man. She had to work hard, for long hours. Yet all the time, throughout the day as she worked, she prayed and fasted. Even at night, she slept little. She often stood praying as dawn broke and her daily tasks began.

One hot night, Rabia's master found he could not sleep. He got up, and walked over to the window of his room. He looked down, into the courtyard below.

There, he saw the solitary figure of Rabia, his slave. Her lips moved in prayer, and he could just catch the words in the still night air.

'Oh God, Thou knowest that the desire of my heart is to obey Thee, and if the affair lay with me, I would not rest one hour from serving Thee, but Thou Thyself has set me under the hand of Thy creature. For this reason I come late to Thy service. . .'

There was something very strange about the scene. At first, the master could not quite understand what it was. Then he realized. There was a lamp above Rabia's head. It hung there, quite still – but without a chain. As he watched, its light filled the whole house.

Suddenly, he was afraid. He returned to his bed, and lay awake, thinking of what he had seen. He was certain of only one thing. Such a woman should not be a slave.

In the morning, he called Rabia to him, and spoke to her kindly. He told her he would set her free.

'I beg your permission to depart,' murmured Rabia, and her master agreed at once.

Rabia set off out of the town, deep into the desert. There she lived as a hermit, alone for a while, serving God. Later, she went as a pilgrim to Makkah.

Helena and Louis

The Crusades were wars between Christians and Muslims. They were fought in the Middle East, for nearly 200 years. In 1187 a great ruler, Saladin, led a Muslim army which recaptured Jerusalem from the Christians. This is a story of Saladin.

The fighting had ended some hours before, and dusk had fallen. On the field of battle, shadowy figures moved among the bodies of the dead and dying. The wives and friends of the soldiers had come to look for those who had not returned to the camps.

Helena wandered across the battlefield. She was looking for her husband Louis, but as time passed, and she could not find him, she became quite sure he was dead.

When it was dark, she returned to her tent and lay down next to her young son, weeping quietly.

In the morning, her child too had vanished.

Helena ran from her tent, calling out her child's name. She searched all morning among the tents of the Christian camp, but no one had seen her son. Her heart filled with dread.

She looked across the fields to the Muslim camp. She had heard that the Sultan, Saladin, was merciful. Perhaps her son had been kidnapped. Perhaps Saladin would set him free. . .

Weeping, Helena made her way to the Muslim camp, and the soldiers there took her to Saladin. As she entered his tent, Saladin was conferring with his generals. He looked at the woman in surprise.

'Mighty Sultan!' pleaded Helena, falling on her knees. 'Help me! My husband was lost in battle and now my child has gone. If your soldiers have the boy, I beg you to release him, for he is all I have!'

Saladin was moved, and ordered his soldiers to search for the child. They soon found him – safe, but frightened, wandering at the edge of the camp.

Helena was overjoyed, and cried out when she saw her son. Outside the tent, a Crusader prisoner was being escorted across the camp, and he heard her.

'Let me see her!' he cried, tearing himself free from his guards and forcing his way into the tent.

Helena could not believe her eyes. For here before her stood Louis! A minute ago she had neither husband nor son – yet now she had them both in her arms again.

Moved by what he saw, Saladin was merciful, and freed Louis at once. Helena fell on her knees once more, this time to thank the Sultan.

'I showed mercy because I must,' Saladin told her. 'My religion tells me that, as Allah is merciful, so must all Muslims be, and so I show mercy to you.'

Abu Ghiyath and the Rich Young Man

There was once a poor man named Abu Ghiyath, who lived in the city of Makkah. He was so poor that he had only one set of clothes to wear, and his family was often short of food.

It was the first day of Ramadan, the month of fasting. Abu Ghiyath sat in the shade of a tree, and stared out at the deserted city streets. Nothing moved. Everyone else was indoors, sheltering from the fierce heat of the afternoon sun.

Abu Ghiyath was deep in thought. He was worried. His family had not eaten for two days. They wore only rags. He had no money, and could do nothing for them.

He trailed his fingers through the sandy soil, drawing pictures in the earth as he pondered his sad plight.

Suddenly, he felt something hard, half buried in the sand. A snake! He stiffened in fear.

But the object did not move. It could not be alive. He brushed the sand away and saw that it was a money belt.

Abu Ghiyath opened the belt, and looked inside. It was filled with gold pieces – a thousand dinars!

So much money! Abu Ghiyath began to dream. What could he do with such a sum? He could buy food for his family, and clothes. . . it would last for years!

But no. The money belonged to someone, surely, and it would not be right to keep it. Even though his children were hungry, and the money probably belonged to someone who was already very rich. . .

Abu Ghiyath argued with himself for some time, and then he picked up the belt and, concealing it among his own clothes, made his way to the Ka'aba, the sacred stone building in the centre of Makkah. There he heard a man calling out:

'I've lost a thousand dinars! If anyone has found it, please tell me!'

Abu Ghiyath went up to him and said:

'The people here are very poor. You should offer a reward for the return of your money. That way, you would encourage the finder to return it.'

'What sort of reward?' asked the man. 'How much?'

'Oh, I think a hundred dinars would be about right,' said Abu Ghiyath.

'Don't be ridiculous,' said the man. 'That's far too much money.'

The next day, Abu Ghiyath was at the Ka'aba again, and again heard the man asking if anyone had found his money.

'You won't get anywhere,' he told him, 'unless you offer a reward. How about ten dinars?'

'No chance,' said the man. 'People should be honest without a reward.'

The third day, the man was at the Ka'aba again, still looking for his money.

'If you offered just one dinar,' said Abu Ghiyath, 'the finder could spend half of it on water for the pilgrims, and half on food for his family.'

'Go away,' said the man. 'There's no reward.'

The next day, Abu Ghiyath approached the man at the mosque.

'Come with me,' he said. 'I have found your money, and I will give it to you.'

The man followed Abu Ghiyath to his house, and took the money belt without a word. He emptied out the coins and counted them carefully, to make sure they were all there. Then he marched away, without even a word of thanks.

A few days later, Abu Ghiyath sat under the tree again, hungrier and more ragged and worried than ever. A shadow fell across his face, and he looked up. There was the man again, standing next to him.

'What's the matter?' snapped Abu Ghiyath. 'What do you want? The money was all there, wasn't it?'

'My father has died,' said the man, quietly. 'He left three thousand dinars, and said I must give a third of it to a poor man, as a charity. I have never met anyone who deserved it as much as you.'

And so it was that Abu Ghiyath's patience and honesty were rewarded, and he was at last able to feed his hungry family.

The Two Brothers

This is a story of two brothers who owned a farm. They shared all the work, and at harvest time, it was their custom to divide the crops between them. Each had exactly the same amount.

The two brothers shared everything equally – though one was married and had children, and the other was a single man.

One night, just after they had gathered in an especially good harvest, the unmarried brother lay awake, thinking of their good fortune.

'But you know, it isn't really fair,' he said to himself. 'My brother has a wife and family to feed, and I have only myself. He should really have a larger share. But I know he won't let me give him anything. So I'll move some of my crops into his store tonight, while it's too dark for him to see me.'

So he got up, and crept out of the house and, very quietly, moved six sacks of corn from his own grain store and into his brother's.

Later that night, the married brother woke up, and he too thought about the harvest.

'What a lucky man I am,' he said to himself. 'I have a lovely family who care for me, and more than enough food for them. But my poor brother! He has no wife and no children. The least I can do is give him some of my corn. But he would never take it. I'll have to move it by night, so he doesn't see me.'

So he too got up, and went to his grain store, and he too moved six sacks of corn and put them in his brother's store.

The next morning, the two brothers got up and went about their business. Imagine the surprise of the unmarried brother, when he went into his store! For there were just as many sacks as on the day before.

'But surely I moved some. . .' he thought. 'How strange. Perhaps I dreamed it. . .'

The married brother was also puzzled. He too had exactly the same number of sacks as the day before.

'And yet I'm sure I moved some,' he said to himself.

Neither brother wanted to mention what he had done, for neither wanted to show off his generosity.

But from that year onwards, every harvest time, each brother moved six sacks of grain into the other's store. And every year, the next morning, each one was amazed to find that the number of sacks in his store remained exactly the same.

And neither of them ever found out why.

A Dinner of Smells

Nasrudin the mullah (or teacher) is a well-known and much-loved folk hero throughout the Muslim world. Sometimes he seems foolish, but really he is wise. Stories like this one are told from China to Africa, and beyond.

Once, long ago, a very fine and expensive restaurant stood on a busy street in a bustling market town.

One day, a poor man passed by this restaurant. He was tired and hungry, for he had had nothing to eat all day. His nostrils caught the smell of the delicious food being cooked inside. He stopped and sniffed, smiled sadly, and began to walk away.

But he did not get far. The owner of the restaurant came storming out into the street.

'Come here!' he bellowed. 'I saw that! You took the smell of my food, and you'll have to pay for it!'

The poor man did not know what to do.

'I cannot pay!' he stammered. 'I have no money!'

'No money!' shouted the restaurant owner. 'We'll see about that! You're coming with me to the Qadi!'

A Qadi is a judge in a Muslim court. Naturally, he is very powerful, and the poor man was frightened.

'Hmm,' said the Qadi, when he had heard the story. 'Well, this *is* an unusual case. Let me think. Come back tomorrow, and I'll pronounce the sentence.'

What could the poor man do? He knew that whatever sum the Qadi demanded, payment would be impossible.

All night long he tossed and turned, unable to sleep for worry. When dawn came he said his prayers and, tired and dejected, made his way to the Qadi's court.

As he passed the mosque he spotted a familiar figure – Nasrudin the mullah. Suddenly, his heart lifted. For he knew that Nasrudin was a clever man, who was sure to be able to think of a way around the problem. He poured out his story, and Nasrudin agreed to come to the court and speak for him.

The rich restaurant owner was already at the court, chatting with the Qadi. The poor man saw that they were friends, and feared the judgement would go against him.

He was right. The Qadi began heaping insults upon the poor man as soon as he saw him, and ordered him to pay a very large sum of money.

At once, Nasrudin stepped forward.

'My lord,' he said to the Qadi. 'This man is my brother. Allow me to pay in his place.'

Then the mullah took a small bag of coins from his belt and held it next to the rich man's ear. He shook the bag, so that the coins jingled.

'Can you hear that?' asked Nasrudin.

'Of course,' the man replied, impatiently.

'Well, that is your payment,' said the mullah. 'My brother has smelled your food, and you have heard his money. The debt is paid.'

And, in the face of such argument, the case was settled and the poor man went free.

Nasrudin and the Glutton

This is another story about Nasrudin the mullah. This version comes from western China – but, as with all Nasrudin stories, it can be enjoyed by anyone, anywhere – and it has something to tell us all.

Long ago in China, there lived a very rich lord. His house and garden were famous throughout the land for their grandeur and beauty. His clothes were so fine that, as he walked by, people gasped in wonder.

You might think that such a wealthy man would spare a thought now and again for others less fortunate than himself. He might, perhaps, have given alms to the poor, or helped the orphan children of the town. But no, he preferred to do nothing at all.

This meant he was often very bored so he spent his time trying to think of new ways to amuse himself. And one day, he decided to play a trick on Nasrudin. For he knew that the mullah blamed him for being selfish and lazy, and he wanted above all to make Nasrudin look foolish.

He sent his servants out to buy a great many large, sweet melons. Then he invited a large number of people to a feast – including, of course, Nasrudin.

When the guests were seated, the servants brought in the melons, and the rich man urged them to eat. 'Eat your fill, friends!' he said. 'There is plenty more.'

The guests needed no encouragement. They did not often have a feast such as this, and they were determined to make the best of it.

As they ate, the heaps of melon skins grew taller on each plate. Surreptitiously, the rich man (who had eaten more than anyone else) slipped all his melon skins on to Nasrudin's plate.

When all the melons were eaten, the guests sat back, patting their stomachs, satisfied with their meal.

The rich man looked about the table and smiled. This was the moment for his joke.

'Look!' he cried, pointing to Nasrudin's plate and the enormous pile of melon peels. 'This man is the greediest person here – though he teaches us to be generous and kind! Yet he goes and eats more melons than the rest of us put together! What a glutton!'

Everyone began to laugh – even the mullah. But as the laughter died away, Nasrudin said quietly:

'But glutton as I may be, I am not the worst one here. For look, I have eaten only the fruit, and I have left the peels uneaten. But our host here – he's eaten everything – peels and all!'

And the rich man hung his head in shame.

43

Background Notes

Zamzam, the Well of Ishmael

This story appears in the Bible, and is told in both the Christian and Jewish tradition, as well as in Islam.

For Muslims, Abraham is an important figure, and one of a long line of prophets who include Noah, Moses and Jesus, as well as Muhammad himself, the last of the prophets.

The well lies near the Ka'aba, the holy cube-shaped building in the centre of Makkah, This was, it is believed, built by Abraham as a place where the One God was to be worshipped.

The story goes that, after many years, the Well of Ishmael fell into disuse and was covered by sand. The holy place where it had been was used as a temple for idols. Many years later, in response to a dream, a man named Abd al-Muttalib dug through the sand to reach the well again. Abd al-Muttalib was the grandfather of the Prophet Muhammad.

The Prophet's Childhood

Muhammad's mother died when he was only six, and he was cared for by his grandfather, Abd al-Muttalib. He was a highly respected and holy man, the keyholder of the Ka'aba (see above) and the keeper of the Well of Ishmael. He died when he was 90 years old and his son, Abu Talib, took charge of Muhammad.

Bahira the Monk

In this story we come across Abu Talib for the first time. He was a rich and respected merchant in Makkah and, most importantly, he was the Prophet's uncle and cared for him as an orphaned child. After the Prophet's revelation, Abu Talib became a devoted follower of the Prophet, but it was his son, Ali, the Prophet's young cousin and later his son-in-law, who was the first man to be converted to Islam.

The First Revelation

This story tells of the beginning of the Holy Qur'an and is central to Islam. Following this vision, the Prophet had many more throughout his life. These visions gave him all the words of the Qur'an.

The story explains that Muhammad told the Angel, 'I cannot read'. The miracle of the Revelation lies in this fact – for Muhammad was illiterate, yet at once started reciting the stories of the prophets, and was able to give moral instructions in language so beautiful and refined that it is universally admired by scholars of Arabic, whatever their religion.

In this story we read of the Prophet's wife, Khadija, who was the very first person to be converted to Islam.

The Hijrah to Madinah

Abu Bakr, who is important to this story, was one of the Prophet's first companions. He was a wealthy and respected man who put all his goods at the disposal of Islam. Later, he became the Prophet's father-in-law, for Khadija died and the Prophet married Abu Bakr's daughter, Aisha.

The Quraysh were the leading tribe of all Arabia, as they had possession of the Ka'aba. This was the cultural and religious heart of Arabia, even before Islam. Since the time of Abraham, it had become a place where idols were worshipped and poets gathered. The Quraysh were divided into ten clans. The two prominent ones were those of Umaya and Hashim – this last being the Prophet's own clan. The Quraysh opposed Islam for eight years as it went against their political and financial interests. In the end however, they embraced it.

Abu Jahl, the leader of the plotters was a man with great commercial and financial interests and felt very threatened by the social reforms that came with Islam. He was eventually killed in battle.

Salman the Persian

The story of Salman's meeting with the Prophet is only the beginning of a life devoted to his service. Salman was responsible for saving the Prophet and his followers a few years later, when the city of Madinah came under siege from enemies of the Muslims. He suggested that they should build a ditch or trench around the city, which the enemy troops would be unable to cross. The plan worked, and the enemies were defeated in a confrontation known as the Battle of the Ditches.

Salman was remembered for his part in this triumph, and also for the fact that he was such a loyal follower of Islam that the Prophet accepted him as one of his family.

Bilal, the First Muezzin

Umaya, Bilal's owner, was a rich and influential landowner, whose descendents became the principal clan of the Quraysh and governed the Islamic empire from CE 661 to 750.

The Prophet's Helpers mentioned here are the Muslims of Madinah who gave shelter and assistance to the Muslims who migrated from Makkah, following the Hijrah to Madinah in CE 622.

Rabia the Slave

Rabia was a famous mystic who lived between CE 713 and 801. As the story tells us, she was freed and devoted herself to God, retiring to a life of seclusion and celibacy. She gathered a number of disciples and many miracles are attributed to her. She was also a poet.

Helena and Louis

The Crusades were fought in the early Middle Ages. In these so-called 'holy' wars, Christians fought against Muslims in order to free Jerusalem and other holy places so that Christian pilgrims could visit them. (Although Jerusalem is, of course, also holy to Muslims.)

Christians have tended to portray Saladin as a cruel and ruthless leader, but historical evidence and Muslim tradition tell a different story, as shown here.

Abu Ghiyath and the Rich Young Man

In many Muslim countries, there is a tradition that in finding something, one may keep it, unless the owner claims it. This lends weight to Abu Ghiyath's argument with himself – but in the end, honesty prevails.

The Two Brothers

Giving to charity is one of the five basic duties of every Muslim, but it should be done without advertisement. The two brothers give in the best possible way, in secret, under cover of darkness.

A Dinner of Smells

The figure of the mullah Nasrudin appears in folk tales throughout the Muslim world. The stories are usually told simply for fun, but this is more serious. Allah is just – but justice is not a matter simply of laws. It is a demand from God that we treat others as we would be treated ourselves.

Nasrudin and the Glutton

This story is Chinese in origin, and again has something to say about the way we treat our neighbours. Ridiculing them is not endearing!

A note about spelling and dates

Arabic has its own alphabet, and the English versions of Arabic words can be spelled in several ways. In this book we have chosen the English spelling which is the closest match between the original Arabic sounds and English sounds, so you will see Makkah instead of Mecca.

Because of the Christian nature of the terms BC and AD, we have referred to dates as BCE or CE: that is Before the Common Era and Common Era.